Jan Thornhill

Before & After

A Book
of Nature
Timescapes

~

Owl

Owl Books are published by Greey de Pencier Books Inc.,
370 King St. West, Suite 300, Toronto, Ontario M5V 1J9

The Owl colophon is a trademark of Owl Children's Trust Inc.
Greey de Pencier Books Inc. is a licensed user of trademarks of Owl Children's Trust Inc.

Text and illustrations © 1997 Jan Thornhill

This book was published with the generous support of
the Canada Council and the Ontario Arts Council.

Canadian Cataloguing in Publication Data
Thornhill, Jan
Before & After: a book of nature timescapes

ISBN 1-895688-61-2

1. Habitat (Ecology) – Juvenile literature. 2. Landscape
changes – Juvenile literature. 3. Time – Juvenile
literature. 4. Picture puzzles – Juvenile literature.
I. Title. II. Title: Before and after.

QH541.14.T46 1997   j574.5'26   C96-932527-4

Design & Art Direction: Julia Naimska

Other books by Jan Thornhill
The Wildlife ABC: A Nature Alphabet
The Wildlife 1 2 3: A Nature Counting Book
A Tree in a Forest
Crow and Fox and Other Animal Legends
Wild in the City

Printed in Hong Kong

A   B   C   D   E   F

A word before *Before & After* begins

Have you ever spotted a bird on a tree branch, and the next time you looked it was gone? Or watched a little kitten grow from a tiny fluff ball into a full-sized cat? As time passes, all living things change. They move with the wind, or grow bigger, or change color. Plants flower and grow fruit. Animals eat, move from one place to another, and have babies. Some changes are easy to see, but others you really have to look for.

In this book, you'll find pictures of special places all over the world. Each place is shown twice: before (like the picture above), and then after time has passed (like the picture below). Find all the animals in the first picture, then turn to the second picture and figure out how things have changed. Look closely—there are lots of surprises!

You'll find *Nature Notes* at the end of the book that will tell you even more about what is hidden in these pictures. I've called these paintings nature timescapes because of the ways that time changes nature's landscapes all over the world—from the deepest forest to your own school yard.

— Jan Thornhill

Butterfly Fish   Sea Snake   Sea Horse   Goby   Clownfish

Jellyfish

Nautilus

Triggerfish

Lobster

Ornate Starfish

Giant Clam

Moray Eel

Before

Porcupine Fish Angelfish Sweetlips Stingray Shark

Sea Turtle

Trumpetfish

Octopus

Blue Starfish

Parrotfish

Sea Urchin

TROPICAL CORAL REEF

Butterfly Fish   Sea Snake   Sea Horse   Goby   Clownfish

Jellyfish

Nautilus

Triggerfish

Lobster

Ornate Starfish

Giant Clam

Butterfly Fish   Moray Eel

After a few seconds

Porcupine Fish   Angelfish   Sweetlips   Stingray   Shark

Sea Turtle

Trumpetfish

Octopus

Blue Starfish

Parrotfish

Sea Urchin

TROPICAL CORAL REEF

Hippopotamus
Baboon
Hyena
Impala
Cape Buffalo
Leopard
Gnu
Marabou Stork
Jackal
Vulture
Lioness

Before

Oxpecker   Cheetah   Ibis   Hornbill

Elephant

Warthog

Zebra

Flamingo

Crested Crane

Giraffe

SAVANNAH

Cape Buffalo

Leopard

Gnu

Marabou Stork

Jackal

Vulture

Hippopotamus   Baboon   Hyena   Impala

Lioness

After a minute

Oxpecker Cheetah Ibis Hornbill

Elephant

Warthog

Zebra

Flamingo

Crested Crane

Giraffe

SAVANNAH

Pygmy Possum   Kangaroo   Cuscus   Papilio Butterfly

Python

Lorikeet

Stick Insect

Koala

Gecko

Sugar Glider

Before

Cockatoo Hawk Moth Kookaburra Marsupial Mouse

Parrot

Tree Frog

Frogmouth

Fruit Bat

Tree Kangaroo

Cicada

FOREST EDGE

Pygmy Possum   Kangaroo   Cuscus   Papilio Butterfly

Python

Lorikeet

Stick Insect

Koala

Gecko

Sugar Glider   Kangaroo   Cuscus   Papilio Butterfly

After *a few minutes*

Cockatoo   Hawk Moth   Kookaburra   Marsupial Mouse

Parrot

Tree Frog

Frogmouth

Fruit Bat

Tree Kangaroo

Cicada

FOREST EDGE

Raccoon   Firefly   Red-winged Blackbird   Bittern   Mayfly

Bullfrog

Water Strider

Perch

Turtle

Minnow

Moose

Before

Mosquito   Sparrow   Dragonfly   Heron   Wood Duck

Spring Peeper

Star-nosed Mole

Leopard Frog

Otter

Water Snake

WETLAND

Raccoon   Firefly   Red-winged Blackbird   Bittern   Mayfly

Bullfrog

Water Strider

Perch

Turtle

Minnow

Moose

After an hour

Mosquito   Sparrow   Dragonfly   Heron   Wood Duck

Spring Peeper

Star-nosed Mole

Leopard Frog

Otter

Water Snake

WETLAND

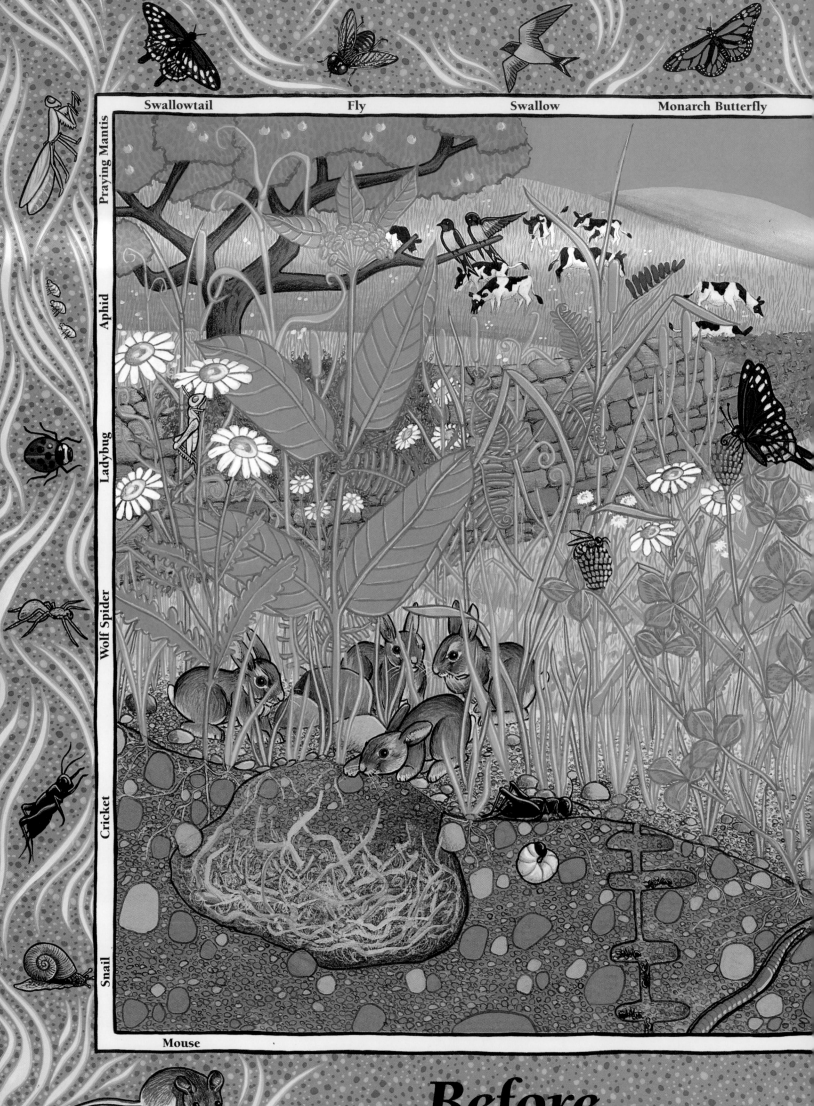

Swallowtail   Fly   Swallow   Monarch Butterfly

Praying Mantis

Aphid

Ladybug

Wolf Spider

Cricket

Snail

Mouse

Before

Kestrel

Pheasant

Cow

Orb Weaver Spider

Honeybee

Grasshopper

Rabbit

Ant

Earthworm

Beetle Larva

MEADOW

Swallowtail   Fly   Swallow   Monarch Butterfly

Praying Mantis

Aphid

Ladybug

Wolf Spider

Cricket

Snail

Mouse

After a day

Kestrel   Pheasant   Cow   Orb Weaver Spider

Honeybee
Grasshopper
Rabbit
Ant
Earthworm
Beetle Larva

MEADOW

Jaguar   "88" Butterfly   Toucan   Tamandua Anteater

Kinkajou

Hummingbird

Poison-arrow Frog

Potoo

Leafcutter Ant

Motmot

Spider Monkey

Before

Vine Snake   Morpho Butterfly   Sloth   Leaf-footed Bug

Howler Monkey

Leaf Katydid

Coatimundi

Iguana

Squirrel Monkey

Macaw

RAIN FOREST

Jaguar   "88" Butterfly   Toucan   Tamandua Anteater

Kinkajou

Hummingbird

Poison-arrow Frog

Potoo

Leafcutter Ant

Motmot

Spider Monkey

After a month

Vine Snake   Morpho Butterfly   Sloth   Leaf-footed Bug

Howler Monkey

Leaf Katydid

Coatimundi

Iguana

Squirrel Monkey

Macaw

RAIN FOREST

Cecropia Moth   Cecropia Caterpillar   Mourning Dove   Wren

Finch

Red Admiral

Cardinal

Toad

Hummingbird Moth

Blue Jay

Human

Before

Pigeon

Gull

Swallowtail

Sparrow

Robin

Fiery Searcher

Squirrel

Starling

Cat

Hummingbird

SCHOOL YARD

Cecropia Moth   Cecropia Caterpillar   Mourning Dove   Wren

Finch

Red Admiral

Cardinal

Toad

Hummingbird Moth

Blue Jay

Human

After a year

Pigeon   Gull   Swallowtail   Sparrow

Robin

Fiery Searcher

Squirrel

Starling

Cat

Hummingbird

SCHOOL YARD

NATURE NOTES

Time brings changes big and small to environments all over the world.
Here are some of the changes you've seen in this book. What's happening with
the rest of the animals in the pictures? Each has a story to tell about life on our planet.

TROPICAL CORAL REEF

A lot can happen in a few seconds in a tropical
coral reef in the Indo-Pacific. A **moray eel** snatches an
unsuspecting **butterfly fish** in its sharp-toothed jaws. Startled
by the appearance of a **shark**, a **porcupine fish** gulps water to
inflate itself like a spiky balloon, while tiny **gobies** dart to safety
among the branches of a coral. A **triggerfish** breaks the sharp
spines off **sea urchins** before eating their soft insides. Leaving
the camouflage of the sandy ocean floor, a **stingray** flaps away.
A **clownfish** lives unharmed among the poisonous tentacles
of a **sea anemone**. A **trumpetfish** shoots from its hiding
place to suck a goby into its mouth.

WETLAND

In an hour, the sun sets and night embraces a
North American wetland. A **moose** and her calf rise
from their resting spot in the tall reeds to eat water lilies in the
early evening. Baby **wood ducks** leave their nest hole in a tree
for the first time, and paddle beside their mother while she looks
for a log where they can spend the night. A **water snake** lies
still, digesting the **leopard frog** it has caught and eaten. A
mayfly flits off after emerging from its nymph shell,
tempting a hungry **perch**. A **bullfrog** and a
spring peeper inflate their throats with
air, filling the night with song.

SAVANNAH

On the plains of an African savannah, a wide
variety of animals gather to drink at a water hole. A
hunting **lioness** crouches hidden in the grass, waiting for the
perfect moment to pounce—less than a minute later, she is down
the hill. Panic-stricken **impalas**, **zebras**, and **giraffes** run for
their lives. **Oxpeckers** stop picking and eating insects off a
warthog's back and fly away. A **hippopotamus**, unafraid, yawns.
Far in the distance, **vultures** and a **jackal** wait for a **hyena**
to eat its fill from the carcass of a **zebra**, while a speeding
cheetah takes an impala down to the ground.

MEADOW

From one day to the next, subtle changes occur in
a meadow. A **mouse** gives birth to pink, hairless babies.
A brooding **pheasant's** eggs hatch and her chicks leave the
nest, staying close by her side as she shows them food. **Wolf
spiderlings** emerge from a portable egg-case and hitch a ride
on their mother's back; a **monarch** butterfly tries its new wings.
While new lives begin, others end. A **fly** escapes the web of an
orb weaver spider to be snatched from the air the next day
by a **praying mantis**. **Ants** swarm a **cricket** weak from
disease, and carry it to their underground nest.

FOREST EDGE

In the wet season, daily rains soak the forest
edge in eastern Australia. But after a downpour the
sun shines again in a few minutes. Most Australian mammals are
marsupials—the young are carried by their mothers in a pouch.
Sugar glider babies, too big for their mother's pouch, ride piggy-
back as she sails between trees. The young of a **marsupial
mouse** cling to her back, as she snatches up a newly
emerged **cicada** before its wings are strong enough to
carry it away. A **tree kangaroo** uncurls and her joey
peeks out from her belly pouch. Non-marsupial
fruit bats unfurl their wings to dry
themselves in the hot sun.

RAIN FOREST

In a South American rain forest, there are many
changes in a month. A baby **spider monkey** and two
young **squirrel monkeys** leave the safety of their mothers' backs
to climb on their own. A young **tamandua anteater** now can
catch **leafcutter ants** with its sticky tongue, and a baby **three-
toed sloth** clings by its claws to a branch. A **coatimundi** gives
birth to three tiny kits, and the tadpoles of a **poison-arrow frog**
develop into small frogs. The eggs of a **potoo**, a **toucan**, and
a **hummingbird** hatch, and the fledglings are
almost ready to fly. A young male **motmot**
has preened feathers from his long tail,
so it looks a bit like a tennis racquet.

SCHOOL YARD

In some environments, a year brings changes
that are hard to see. But when the **human** animal has a
hand in things, great changes can happen. In one year, an
almost lifeless cement school yard is transformed into an oasis
buzzing with life. Feeders attract many birds, such as the **blue
jay**, **cardinal**, **mourning dove**, and **finch**. A **wren** finds a bird-
house a safe place to lay her eggs, and shrubs provide hidden
nooks for other nesting birds. Flowers produce nectar for
hummingbirds, and for **swallowtail** and **red admiral**
butterflies. A half-buried flowerpot is an instant
house for a **toad**.